Islam and
Globalization

Islam and Globalization

A Contemporary Vision

Calling for
Dialogue, Peace and Brotherhood,
Rejecting Terrorism and Extremism

ELTAYEB ALI ABDELRAHMAN

To order additional copies of this book, contact:
Xlibris Corporation
1-888-795-4274
www.Xlibris.com
Orders@Xlibris.com
60191

Contents

◊ Dedication 7

◊ Acknowledgment 9

◊ Preface 11

◊ The Islamic State 13

◊ Concept of the Islamic Nation 16

◊ Contribution of Islam to Civilization(An Example of Universality
and Globalizations) 20

◊ The setting of the best Centuries 24

◊ Islam Confrontation to Extremism and Terrorism 26

◊ Intermediateness of Islam 34

◊ Between universality of Islam and Globalization 39

◊ Glossary 45

◊ References 47

For all the honest
and the good people

Acknowledgment

I *wish to convey my thanks to my colleagues and friends:*

♦ Mr. Mohammed Ahmed Hamdoon.
♦ Mr. Beshir Suliman.
♦ Mr. Elsir Khider Sid Ahmed.
♦ Madam Alzulfa Mustafa.
♦ Mr. Osama ElKhatim Elkarib.

For their kind assistance in translating, revising and typing this book

Eltayeb A. Abdelrahman
Ministry of Culture
And Information
Wad-Medani
Gezira State
R.SUDAN

Preface

S ince man was created, rightness and falsity, goodness and evil have been conflicting; this would certainly continue since man exists on the Earth; the fact which conforms with Islam itself, which since its emergence continuous battles have been waged against falsehood-such falsehood that uses all available weapons to wipe out the features of the rightness and truth of Islam.

Despite the fact that Islam is the last religion to shut off the Divine Messages, but it has been exposed since its emergence, and still is, to many stirred attacks and suspicions concerning the Islamic belief and teachings according to history books and current events.

It is worth mentioning that Islam has never denied any of the previous prophets, nor what had been revealed and descended to them from heaven with regard to the sacred books. Moreover, it has never compelled any of the followers of the previous heavenly religions to follow its creed. Furthermore, this matter has never been confined to non-denial people, but also Islam made clear that faith in all the Prophets of God and the Books descended to them are basic factors of every Muslim's belief; and without this belief it would be incorrect according to the tolerant situation of Islam in regard to the previous religions, which we hope that it should be met with a parallel tolerance, so that the number of those who are against Islam should be decreased. In fact, what happened was absolutely contrary to what was expected. Obviously, attacks from all corners occurred and none of the other religions has been exposed to such attacks. We perceive that part of this disfigurement of Islam was caused by some ill-misbehaved Muslims in the name of Islam. And Off course, Islam is irresponsible for their act.

This call of Islam and globalization which we introduce is a call for keeping away Islam from any possible confrontation and conflict between the world civilizations. Apparently, it's a call for dialogue between Islam and the other religions; and this sprouts out from the fact that the Islamic Nation is an intermediate one calling for justice and equity among all people of the world, because Muslims are – like others – sons of the same planet, sharing the same resources and destiny. Not only that but also Muslims always call for a strong human brotherhood, and mutual support which invites for tolerance and co-existence between civilizations, and, consequently, we should not come into clashes favoring the original human goodness embodied in the teachings and values of Islam as an evidence of what has been stated above.

The Islamic Conference for Dialogue which was held in June2008 under the kind sponsorship of the Servant of the Two Holly Sanctuaries His Highness King Abdalla Al Saaud in Mecca as an outburst of an Islamic Dialogue consolidating with the peoples of the world and the followers of other religions and cultures starting from the legal and ethical international relations basis to conduct a dialogue on the campaigns confronting Islam and its leading symbols, and all Muslims who are spreading all over the world comprising one fifth of mankind need to be considered, and respected and that such campaigns which contempt religions and hatred that stir disorder among the peoples of the world must hopefully be stopped. This matter is so crucial that 500 international outstanding figures of different Islamic doctrines had been invited to conduct a wide dialogue within the Islamic sphere first in preparation for conducting a comprehensive dialogue with other civilizations in order to discuss all the issues raised related to the common human concerns to avoid any clash of civilizations and to lessen the degree of confrontations between the followers of religions, and to open frank discussions managed to surpass many obstacles laid down by extremists who were described by King Abdalla as Narrow-minded, and who are incapable of seeing the believers of other religions, only as suicide targets causing the death of innocent people whom God forbade killing them.

We Muslims long to seeing our call based on the love of the people, and a call for rightness, goodness and beauty.

We are preachers of righteousness living in peace with other people and rejecting war.

So, why don't others look to us in a perspective of tolerance grounded on the idea of dialogue and not clashing so as to keep our earthly world ever wonderful.?

This conference will be followed by an international Inter-Faith Conference in Spain in July (2008).

All religions will be invited to attend so as to come to common terms, and to activate religions co-existence to be a reality and to maintain international peace and order, and to blockade the narrow-minded who abused the innocent Islam of their extremism and wrong understanding of true Islam.

THE ISLAMIC STATE

One can not be regarded a Muslim till he pronounces the two testimonies of Islam, Allah (God) Almighty says:

(The true Believers are only those,
Who believe in
The oneness of Allah and His
Messenger (Muhammed) (peace be upon him)
Su´ra: An-Nur (62)

• *PURPOSE*

So the purpose of the Islamic State is Built on:
The foundation of Tawheed*
(The Oneness of God), and the, *Recognition of the prophethood of Muhammed.

The Holy Qur'an states that the aim and purpose of this state is to establish maintenance and development of those virtues with which the Creator of this universe wishes for the prevention and eradication of all evils, whose presence in human life is utterly abhorrent to God. The state of Islam is not intended for a political administration only, nor for the fulfillment of the collective will of any particular set of people; rather, Islam places a high ideal before the state and for the achievement of which it must use all possible means at its disposal. And this purpose includes the qualities of purity, beauty, goodness, virtue, success and prosperity which God wants to flourish in the life of His creatures and which should be engendered and evolved and that all the kind exploitation, injustice, and disorders which, in the view of God, are ruinous for the world and detrimental to the life of His creatures are suppressed and prevented. Simultaneously, by placing before us this high ideal, Islam gives us a clear outline of its moral system. And it states desired virtues and the undesirable evils. Keeping this outline in view, the Islamic State can plan its welfare program through ages and under any conditions.

The persistent demand made by Islam is shown in the principles of morality which must be observed at all costs and in all the walks of life. Hence, it lays down an unalterable policy for the state to base its politics on justice, truth and honesty. It is not prepared, under any circumstance whatsoever, to tolerate fraud, falsehood and injustice for the sake of any political, administrative or national expediency. Whether it is the mutual relations of the rulers and the ruled within the state, or the relations of the state with other states, precedence must always be given to truth, honesty, and justice against material consideration ; it imposes similar obligations on the state as on the individual, viz., to fulfill all contracts and obligations, to maintain uniform measures and standards for dealings; to remember duties along with the rights of others when expecting them to fulfill their obligations; to use power and authority for establishing justice and for perpetrating justice; to look upon duty as sacred obligations and to fulfill it scrupulously; and to regard power as the trust of God and to use it with the belief that one has to render an account of one's actions to Him in the Hereafter.

• *FUNDAMENTAL RIGHTS*

Although an Islamic state may be set up in any part of the earth, Islam does not seek to restrict human rights or privileges to the geographical limits of its own state.

Islam has laid down some universal fundamental rights for humanity as a whole, which are to be observed and respected under all circumstances whether one is resident within the territory of the Islamic state or outside it, or he is in peace or war with the state. Human blood is Sacred as preserved and cannot be spilt without justification. It is impermissible to oppress women, children, old people, sick persons or the wounded. Woman's honor and chastity worth respect under all circumstances. The hungry person must be fed, the naked clothed, and the wounded medically treated irrespective of their belonging to the Muslim community or not, even if they are from its enemies. These and a few other provisions have been laid down by Islam as fundamental rights for any person by virtue of his status as a human being enjoyed under the constitution of an Islamic state. Even the rights of citizenship in Islam are not confined to persons born within the limits of its state but are granted to every Muslim irrespective of his place of birth. A Muslim ipso facto becomes the citizen of an Islamic State as soon as he sets foot on its territory with the intent to live therein and thus enjoy equal rights of citizenship along with those who acquire its citizenship by birthright.

Citizenship should, therefore, be common to all the Islamic states that may exist in the world;

And consequently Muslims need not any passport to enter or depart any of them. So, every Muslim has to be regarded as eligible and fit for all positions that need high responsibilities in an Islamic state without any consideration of race, colour or class.*

Islam has also laid down certain rights for non-Muslims who live within the boundaries of an Islamic state, and these rights must necessarily form part of the Islamic Constitution. According to the Islamic terminology such non-Muslims are Dhimmess (the covenant), implying that the Islamic State has entered into a covenant with them and guaranteed their protection. Life and property are protected exactly equal to a Muslim citizen. There is no difference at all between a Muslim and Dhimmee in respect of the civil or criminal law. The Islamic state shall not interfere with the personal law of the Dhimmees.

They will have full freedom of conscience and belief. *

---

* Some of the points referred to here are to materialize when the Islamic state has attained its final form as far as the territory phase is concerned, efforts will be made to come into close conformity with them as possible. The Islamic state is to be established gradually and will not come into like a bolt from the blue

Concept of the Islamic Nation

This term "Islamic Nation" is different from "Islamic World", that is the "Islamic Nation" would include all the peoples of the earth without any exception since their God is one. The term "Islamic Nation" is more comprehensive than "the Muslim World". The entire globe is the Mumin's "those of strong believe home. That will make a lot of difference in the eye of others – the non-Muslims, for instance. Therefore, all the land is good for Islam Call and to all people no matter be they, black or white and what so ever a language they speak.(it is no man's land). God (Allah) says

"We have not sent thee, But as a universal (messenger) to men, giving them Glad tidings, And warning them (Against sin), but most men understand not"
Su´ra: Saba (28)

The term "Islamic World" is a geographical concept with a limited definition, which means those countries with a majority of Muslims, but the difference is that Islam has made for Muslims a special Nation; that is a Nation of a unique concept and not like any other Nation on Earth. The Muslim's Nation is totally different from all other nations. It's different from the nations that had existed before it. It has its different character. All people are slaves to God and Allah (God) is the only King of the universe. In this, God says

"Verily, this Brotherhood of yours is a single Brotherhood, And I am your lord and cherisher: therefore Serve me (and no other).But (later generations) cut off their a affair (of unity) One from author: (yet) will they all return to us.
Su´ra: Anbiaa (92).

Allah's message was and ever is one, and His Messengers treated it as one and they are brothers of the same Target! It is people of narrower views who come later and trade on the earlier names that break up the Message and the Brotherhood into jarring camps and sects. Allah gives credit for every act of righteousness, however be it small, and when combined with sincere Faith in Allah, it becomes the stepping stone to higher and higher things, it is never lost. But when weakness comes to such a pass that the Wrath of Allah descends as it did on the Village of the children of Israel, Sodom, the case becomes hopeless. The righteous were warned and delivered before the Wrath descended. But those who were destroyed will not get another chance, as they flouted all previous chances, they would only be raised at the approach of the Day of Judgment. For this and other reasons Allah has described such a nation, that of righteousness, as the best of nations that is ginned to people. Allah says'

(ye are the best
Of peoples, evolved
For mankind.
Enjoying what is right,
Forbidding what is wrong,
And believing in God.
If only Uee people of Uee Book
Had faith, it was best
For them: among them
Are some who have faith
But most of them
Are perverted transgressors.)
Su´ra: AL-i-Imran (110).

"People of the Book" is a term given to the Jews and the Christians alike. It is a respectful title mentioned to Muslims in the Qur'an. The Muslims here are commanded to invite – O people of the Book! O learned people! O people who claim to be the recipients of Divine Revelation, of a Holy Scripture, let us gather onto a common platform-

"That we worship. None but Allah "because none but God is worthy of worship. It is along this road that the world can be saved from disaster. The Evil that men do lies after them! Islam in its wider sense means peace and for this peace we should work together and through the help of Allah we can maintain peace and enjoy life, we must look for a true Faith and real revival, but there will be no revival without a religion as is happening in some areas. How can we cure troubles without Faith and good will? We must look for a happy issue with God. Such a revival, if it occurs, will only mean that the hateful features we have against Islam are the real cause of our unhappiness. What the world needs is reasonableness, tolerance, and the realization of the interdependence of the human family. In Islam, this interdependence has been enormously increased by modern inventions and the purely mundane arguments for a kindly attitude to one's neighbour are very much stronger than they were at any earlier time. It is to such considerations that we must look.

In the abstract, the Jews and the Christians would agree to all the three propositions contained in this Quranic Verse but in practice they fail. A part from doctrinal lapses from the unity of One true God, Allah, there is the question of a Consecrated Priesthood, which among the Jews was hereditary also, as if a mere human being could claim superiority apart from his learning and the purity of his life, or could stand between man and God in some special sense, Islam does not only recognize Priesthood!, but, also gives full respect and recognition to Jesus and Christianity which is an obligation to any Muslim. The creed of Islam is given to us here in a Nutshell: says:

"say ye" We believe
In God, and the revelation
Given to us, and to Abraham,
Ismāil,Isaac Jacob,
And the tribes, and that given
To mosses and Jesus, and that given
To (all) Prophets from their Lord:
We make no difference
Between one and another of them:
And we bow to God (in Islam)"
su'ra: Bagara (136).

The Muslim position is therefore, clear indeed. The Muslim does not claim to have religion peculiar to himself, because Islam is not a sect or an ethnic religion, but in its view all Religion is one, for the truth is one; and that it was the same Religion Preached by all the earlier Prophets. It was the Truth taught by all the Inspired Books. In essence it amounts to a consciousness of the Will and Plan of God and joyful Submission to that Will and Plan.

If any one wants a Religion other than that, he will be false to his own Nature, as he is false to God's will and plan.

Such one can not expect guidance and he has deliberately renounced guidance.

Muslims all over the world:

The area dominated by Muslims is estimated over 37 m2 k.m. The dwellers are over a thousand million Muslim (850 million as a majority plus 250 million, as a minority in the world) In spite of the state of hostility and wars against Muslims, the fact remains that an expansion in Muslim countries and population is increasing. It is the Religion of Future. It does expand, because Muslims fight to freedom and for the salvation of man.

Muslim Countries:

Majorities Countries♦

* Africa: 29 countries.
* Asia: 35 countries
* Europe: 35 countries

Minority Countries♦

* Asia: 12 countries
* Africa: 15 countries
* Europe: 12 countries

This is in addition to 3 countries in North, South America and Australia which are countries of small numbers of Muslims.

Contribution of Islam to Civilization

– The Role of Islamic Civilization and its Contributions – :

(An Example of Universality and a Model of Globalization)

N o doubt that the historical facts show that Islam was capable, during a short period since its rising, to establish the oldest wonderful civilization known in history. Truly, that Muslim philosophers were the first to teach the world how the freedom of thought agrees with the proper religion and that we have never seen any nation in history with an outstanding scientific, artistic, linguistic and religions influence like that of the Islamic Nation Scripts and international historical documents would actually show the early impact of the Islamic Nation on Europe during the Middle Ages as a human exposure to such an Islamic contribution to the human civilization. All this came up with the earlier appreciated endeavors of Muslim Scholars who enriched both unknown fields of science and knowledge which were grounded on solid distinguished principles.

As a consequence of the renewable and civilized leading role of Muslims during the "Omeya and Abbasi Dominance", the Islamic civilization managed to introduce an example of universality and a model of globalization characterized by its positive influence on Christian Europe through the gates of civilization in Andalusia, Sicily, Damascus, Fas, Bukhara, Samergund and many other Islamic Capitals. That was because Muslim scholars did not keep the empirical methods which they had invented, but they left wide-opened opportunities to many European students, scholars and researchers to benefit from it. Not only that but also they allowed others to translate various Muslim works in different walks of life, especially, in "Chemistry, medicine, architecture, physics, mathematics, agriculture and sociology etc. Such a translation from Arabic – which was the world language then to European languages particularly into Latin which, in turn, had shared in transferring the scientific Islamic methods and its results. We must not forget the parallel role of the Persians, Indians, Greeks and the Jews during the Abbasi Era – and their efforts in translating the books of legislations, surgery and processing drug . . . etc. Added to this is the role of the monks who had taken initiative to translate Greek sciences into Arabic. Moreover, thousands of Islamic Arab manuscripts enriched many Libraries all over the world. All that was during the Twentieth and the Thirteenth centuries, the impact of which was reflected positively in laying down the foundation for the modern civilization of Europe. So, naturally, that had lead Europe to play a complementary part in human civilization. As far as mathematics is concerned it is worth mentioning that W. Germany had chosen the year 2008 (the German year of Mathematics) that is because, as the Chancellor said; "Mathematics is a common language for all the empirical sciences which transfer many in existing things to facts which is the essence of life." On the other hand, the Chairman of the Germen Union of Mathematicians said: it is the year which will include a historical show for mathematical sciences, its cultural and scientific advancement and, additionally, introducing the most prominent mathematicians. He went on to point out the early role of mathematics on intercommunication between civilizations through the exchange of theories and research between Europe and the Arabs, Muslims, Indians, Greeks and Babylions. He also said with strong emphasis on the role of Arab and Muslim mathematicians during the Middle Ages which coverd different fields of mathematics. He pointed out the unarguable facts about their invention of the figure (0) their contributions to Algebra, Logarithms and Solid Geometry. Not only that but he also considered the impact of Islamic arts and architecture which were connected with Trigonometry to find its way to Europe. That was his message to the New German Generations to deepen the values of openness, tolerance and dialogue with others. It should also be known that the Persians, Indians, Greeks and the Jews have translated from Arabic so many books in different fields of knowledge Islamic teachings, surgery, medicine, composition, and others. In the filed of architecture Muslims had built the most admirable artistic architecture exampled in so many everlasting buildings, some of which are the mosques which Muslims built East and West of the world. From these we can mention: "Gurtuba Mosque" which was built by Abdul Rahman – the first and was finished by his son 'Husham'. It is regarded as one of the most splendid buildings, that is because it was built on (1400) pillars, and that (4700) lanterns plated with gold and silver hang down from its roof which, was covered with cedar wood. Other mosques include Lahour mosque and so many others which scatter along the Islamic Domain, and each of them had its distinguished architecture. From these we can point out:

- Lahour Mosque in India.
- Asfahani Mosque in Persia.
- Al-Azher Mosque and that of Mohamed Ali in Egypt.
- Omer Mosque in Jerusalem, which was built by Abdul Malik Ben Marawan.
- Medina Mosque, and the Great Omayad Mosque built by AL Waleed. In addition to that, the palaces built by Muslims are regarded also as splendid architecture from which we can point out:
- AL Hamra palace in Seville and yards of lions in Granada.
- Abdl Rahman EL Nasir had built AL Zahra Tower as a memorial to his beloved Zahra.
- Many monuments were such as those in ALipo and Damascus which were destroyed by Hulaco, but, the Mongolian Empire had given to the Islamic World the marvelous memorial Taj Mahal.
- In the field of industry, Muslims had their contributions i.e.: – Yahia – one of the Ministers of Aron AlRasheed established the first paper factory in Summergund after utilizing the knowledge of the Chinese captives in the field.
* Muslims also transferred sugar, which they had brought, from India to Europe.

Other Contributions:

- Arabs brought to Europe cosmetics like "Murwad and Kuhul" used for the decoration of the eye. They also took the "Beads . . . Sibha" from India and some other perfumes.
- They used pigeons to carry ciphers and messages to be delivered at long distances.
- In the field of music
  'Al Farabi' was the first to play a musical instrument and the first who used logarithms in composing music. Another man in the field of music was 'Ziriab' who was the first to introduce a fifth string in a musical instrument. He was also the first 'Beatle' with long hair besides being the first person to wear different costumes according to the seasons of the year.
- In the field of literature, there was the famous work (Akber Nama), ELShahnama by EL Ferdoysi. This poem consists of one million and six hundred thousand stanzas, covering 330 volumes, but the Sultan of the "Ottaman Empire" chose only 80 volumes and burnt the rest of them. The poet was very much grieved and migrated to 'Khurasan' where he died. Many other Muslim novelists, dramatists and poets have contributed to

the enrichment of literature, but the most outstanding were the numbered poets who composed the most sweet and pleasant poetry. There were also some famous poetess like "AL Khansaa" and "Al Abbasa".

Not only that, but Islam had many merits on the international heritage of literature and arts e.g.:

- Al Farabi and the Utopia.
- Ibn Tufail and Hay Ben Yeghzan; from which some was taken in Robinson Cruso.
- Ibn Arabi and Abu Al-alla Al Marri and their influence on Dante and his contemporaries.

The setting of the best Centuries

The human environment has a number of unavoidable characteristics for any civilized entity which can never rise without them: because they would secure the co-ordination of social life, and set equilibrium at the following four levels:

♦ The economic, political, cultural and the religious (the ethical), which are all inseparable from each other ; but they blend into and interact in an intricately interwoven manner, yet, the religious characteristic (the ethical) is the fence that surrounds them all, transmitting vividness and animation that would make them all capable to move actively and idealistically in favor of the human communities, that is because any nation is validly exposed to a religious doctrine shown out in beliefs and values whose finger prints are reflected in the general behavior of individuals and the community; bearing in mind that the relationship between religion and morals is a social-born instinct which was and still working for furnishing the equilibrium of necessity of stable values and civilized indentation.

Best Centuries Setting:-

(They are) those who, if we establish them in the land, establish regular prayer and give regular charity, enjoin the right and forbid wrong: with God resets the end (and decision) of (all) affairs) **su´ra : Hajj (41)**

Thus the Islamic Religion was established or, in other words, it has been founded to spread the Islamic Religion ; and consequently, the call has remained a prominent feature of the State, not only that, but also it is one of its major functions and one of its ultimate goals. So, unavoidably, the Islamic State has undergone different events over one thousand years leaving behind the glorious golden centuries, and little by little the State abandoned its message, and unfortunately the call was firstly victimized; and only the Islamic Community remained performing the call.

The Islamic Nation remained stateless, and thought was deeply hampered, then followed by the lack of creed and ethics, together with the destruction of the economic and political systems, and also the social order was apparently devastated, and all this has been associated with the major crime known in the history of Islam and Muslims, resembled in the cancellation of the Califate during the era of the Ottoman Turks Empire, during the reign of K.Atatourk. So the Islamic bond broke up with the military occupation, accompanied by a parallel one of thought and belief through missionary activities and orientalism. And as an effect of this, many countries emerged in existence instead of one Islamic State.

Major Causes of Setting

This was due to the following factors:

1 – The prolongation of the downfall of the State.
2 – The absence of call, misguiding and misleading due to the absence of **Dawa** (preach) along with the separation, incapability, helplessness and reminiscence of Muslims.

Confronting Extremism and Endeavors towards Intermediateness

The Islamic world have witnessed many changes during the last quarter of the Twentieth Centaury which were unknown before, such changes have been widely circulated and spread by those who were calling for (The Return to Islam), and those who think of (The Islamic Political Awakeness),and those who adopted a system of an Islamic Government), and the last who support an (Islamic Revolution) the changes which had spread in different parts of the Islamic world, the reality which had lead contemporary scholars to introduce a new or a renewed statement in response to the wrong allegations made by those who stand under the banners of various Islamic Groups, which prevailed with the Islamic Arena either wrong or right. Some of such issues raised were a reflection of a statement for the relationship between Islam and the existing systems regard to the political and social aspects. Also, parts of these issues were devoted to the situation of the modern Islamic concepts which had been refused by the young Islamic organizations. They had either accepted or adopted them. Further, some of these issues were mere Criticism of the causes, which forced all, or most of them are to be extravagant which is termed: as (Extremism) and violence also, which is termed (Terrorism), and the personal tendency for being fanatic which is termed (Commitment). The Islamic Awakeness played a crucial role in religion for all this good; yet, many affiliated members of the said groups had mixed good and bad deeds with other and that was the fatal reason the Islamic Awakeness have fallen into leading to heresies and making Muslims unbelievers for sheer differences in opinions, doctrines or political commitment, or due to personal behavior. Such heresies had affected even their makers themselves to the extent that some of them had made some others who belong to the same group of unbelievers. Unfortunately, money and blood were proscribed . . . and as a natural consequence for such an act lead to a vertex where the Islamic Nation was put in danger up to this time moment. Personally, I think that such inflexible adoptions and trends are equal to the enmity known before. The appearance of Islam, consequently, both in the East and West have been strongly affected by such new adoptions and trends as corrupt and evil. Offcourse, they miss-judged the civilization of today as inhuman, and by doing so they were wronged grossly.

Undoubtly, no one denies the fact that the Muslims have contributed in making the human civilization through their appreciated impact on science, industry and other natural and theoretical inventions on the various spheres of knowledge of to-day.

So, it is not strange that they forget that the religious diversity of the Islamic Community as solid, an unbreakable source of power and dignity, besides that the peoples of other Books who share with us the sameness of brotherhood and citizenship rights preserved by Islam.

Thus the people of misguidance influenced the uprising generations, a thing that let efforts meet the renewal of knowledge, thought, culture, and the religious belief to limit the influence of such a trend of violence and extravagance as a step for the correct religion to salvate the young people from assaulting dangers of the mislead thought and its distructive results.

In conclusion, so many pious scholars and rational thinkers broke the chain of silence to safeguard the youth through intermediateness which is one of the most outstanding characteristics of Islam, along with ceaseless endeavors towards the dawn of the over domination supremacy and the recession of misguidance and deviation.*

Confronting Extremism Aspiring For Moderation

The Islamic World had witnessed wide spread manifestations which circulated during the last quarter of the Twentieth Century and which were unknown before; but were attributed to those who call for: (THE RETURN TO ISLAM), and those who think of: (THE ISLAMIC POLITICAL AWAKENSS), or those who are interested in: (AN ISLAMIC GOVERNMENT), or (AN ISLAMIC REVOLUTION); such issues which require contemporary scholars, part of which was a reply to the allegations of the numerous Islamic groups which occupied the Islamic arena, and were sometimes wrong or right, and that some of which are explanations of facts concerning the relationship of either political or the social setup between Islam and the existing systems. Some of these issues are the explanations of modern concepts of Islam refused by the young generations of the Islamic organizations, or accepted to deal with, or to make sure of its advantages or disadvantages, or its harm. It is evident now, that some of this was a criticism of the reasons which pushed those young-all or most of them, towards extravagance which is called (EXTREMISM), or(TERRORISM), and between personal alienation of ethics or behavior which is called (FUNDAMENTALISM).

It is true that good can be achieved through the (ISLAMIC AWAKENESS), but many who affiliated from it, had mixed a good deal with a bad one by making people unbelievers which was the worse hearsay of such an act, and so they had fallen into badness only for difference of opinion, or for adopting certain doctrines making people irreligious, or due to the difference of political situation, or due to the personal behavior. It is true now that even the heresy makers themselves were not safe of it, because some of the group members categorized others as irreligious or unbelievers; and the ongoing chain hatch another one, till the heresy went to mistrust their masters (SHEIKHS). The heresy of making people unbelievers was followed by its requirements, most important of which is proscribing blood and money, the situation which put the Islamic Nation, in many countries in a dilemma of which the Nation couldn't get out of it up this moment, because the seeds of bad thought couldn't be rooted out leaving the heresy of making people unbelievers, a legal son of rigidness which attacked different groups : young and old who had some knowledge which pushed them to catch some of the (ISLAMIC AWAKENESS), but they were ignorant, and unable to know that knowledge has so many faces, and that the correct sight has a wide scope. They also forget to remember that The Fathers and Grandfathers since the COMPANIONS of the PROPHET (Peace be upon Him) lived without dyning one to another, not to blame others or belittle them due to the difference of doctrine or of thought and that they always praise them high. Rigidness is a twin pair with bad influence, harmness and deep hatred of:

- Those who were not from the same religion, civilization or culture.
- They categorize the West as all evil.
- That the Western civilization is all corrupt.
- Non-Muslim citizens are from a second class citizens.

But they have forgotten that the human contemporary civilization is neither Eastern or Western, and that Muslims had contributed in its existence from what they had bestowed upon Mankind regard to what Islam had given to civilization. Not only that, but they have forgotten that the religious diversity of the Islamic Community is a source of power, and that the believers of other religions are citizens who have the home and humanitarian brotherhood, and that they have the all rights preserved by Islam and protected by "Sharia" law. So, the people of falsity have influenced the uprising generations. Now the question is how to raise the meaning of Religious Co-Existence? Many efforts have been exerted to renew the statement of knowledge, thought and culture to limit the influence of the trend of extravagance as a step for the revival of the correct religion to save the young from the trap of the abnormal thinking and its consequence ;, the atmost of which is misbehavior.

Many pious scholars, rational thinkers who saved uncountable members have broken silence and taken the initiative to safeguard uncountable numbers of youth from the grip of the extremists and to escape dangers and then direct them towards **(INTERMEDIATNESS)**, which will lead them to the right ideas of Islamic path. Efforts are still carried out aspiring for the supremacy of reason and the recession of deviation.

Islam Against Fanaticism

One of the most prominent Islamic scholars is Sheikh AL-Azhar who whose deep and through knowledge of the Islamic Sharia, had been put up on the top of one of the most outstanding Islamic Academic Organizations, holding the Vice-Chandeorship of AL Azher University in Cairo-Egypt.

About the issue of fanaticism he said : "Islam is a religion which has nothing to do with it, and, consequently, Islam doesn't invite Muslims to practice it, because the sources of Islam which are derived from the Holy Qur'an and the Prophetic Suna doesn't contain anything of that ; and added that the call to Islam-as Qur'an says – is based on the foundation of wisdom, beautiful preaching, and good argument, such methods are ofcourse far away from any type of fanaticism. Islamic Sharia from which the speech of the Prophet *(Peace be upon Him)* is considered the second part of Qur'an said to the unbelievers of Mecca after they refused the call of the Prophet to Islam *(Peace be upon Him)*:

(To you be your way,
And to me mine)
Su´ra: Kafiru´n (6).

Not only that, but Islam call is for the whole people irrespective of their differences, as Qur'an Says:

(O mankind! We created you from a
single (pair) of a male and female,
And made you into Nations and
tribes, that ye may know each other
(Not that ye may despise (Each other).
Verily The most honored of you in
the sight of God
Righteous of you
And God has full knowledge
And is well acquainted
(With all things)
Su´ra: Hujurat (13)

Islam also asks Muslims Straight forwardly and clearly to practice peaceful co-existence with non-Muslims as Qur'an says :

(God forbids you not,
With regard to those who
Fight you not for (your) Faith
Nor drive you out
Of your homes,
From dealing kindly and justly
With them: For God Loveth
Those who are just)
su´ra: Mumtahana (8)

Not only that but Islam calls for forgiveness, condonation, and meeting insult with tolerance based on the probability that the enemy might be a friend, the fact which is well explained in the Holy Qur'an as follows:

(And the remission
Of the man's half
Is the nearest to righteousness
And do not forget
Liberality between yourselves.
For God seas well
All that ye do)
su´ra: Bagara (237)

And in another verse Qur'an confirms the same meaning above as :

Nor can Goodness and Evil
Be equal. Repel (Evil)
With what is better:
Then will he between whom
And these was hatred
Become as it were
Thy friend and intimate)
su´ra: H´a.M´im (34)

And the Prophet *(Peace be upon Him)* confirmed the same meaning too, as he said: "Facilitate and not constrain, announce good and glad news, and don't disaffect". Which is a call to abandon fanaticism that is because disaffections incorporates in fanaticism while good announcement incorporates in tolerance So, Islam rejects fanaticism and therefore it rejects terrorism and frightening those who are peaceful, and killing others, whereas Islam from its overall view considers aggression on a single individual as an aggression on the whole mankind, the Qur'an i.e verse reads:

(A person – unless it be
For murder or for spreading
Mischief in the land-
It would be as if
He if any one saved a life,
It would be as if he saved
The life of the whole people)
su´ra: Māida (35)

In conclusion, it is now clear that the accusation and attribution of fanaticism to Islam don't stand on solid grounds, because it has no evidence from the doctrines of Islam. And, if there are some fanatics, or extremists, or terrorists, that will never be attributed to Islam or its doctrines, but it will be attributed to the wrong awful understanding of the Islamic doctrines. So, Islam must not bear the sins of that, and it is a necessity to differentiate between the good doctrines of Islam and the wrong behaviors of some Muslims.

From another point of view it is true that fanaticism is practiced among other groupes in all religions., while terrorism has become an international phenomena and is not confined to the followers of a particular religion than those of other religions, which has became a meer fact in front of all the eyes of our contemporary world ; the fact which raises an important question: Is it Islam, which has created this international phenomenon between the followers of all religions?

Intermediateness of Islam

I slam is defined as being the five pillars of this religion; The Prophet's *(Peace be upon Him)* was answered by, Gabriel when he asked about religion (Islam) said: "Al-Islam implies that you were witness that there is no god but "Allah" and that Muhammad is the messenger of "Allah", and you establish prayer, pay Zakat, observe the fast of Ramadan, and perform pilgrimage to the House(the Kábah in Mecca), if one has the means to do so*

≈Narrated by Imam-Bukhari and Muslim≈ It is the most outstanding characteristic of the tolerance of Islamic Sharia from which many values emerge: kindness, leniency, easiness in both belief and work. These characteristics maintain the goals and objectives which match with instinct, and that intermediateness is an innocent way of fantasies, heresies and extremism, such characteristics aim to teach and purify the soul to keep it away from fantasies, Satan and the appetite of life. It is for all that correct Islam warns of the deviated trends from both wings:

- The Right Wings: which deal with heresies incorporating overstepping the limits of speech, work and belief.
- The Left Wings: which neglect obligations fulfillment due to remissness.

So, both wings are deviated from the right path, but the perverted who brought it had their heresies, aberrations, suspicions and disorders which led to the division of the Islamic Nation into many subdivisions. But the fact remains that Islam is moderate in all issues i.e.

* Between the present and hereafter life.
* Of faith, ethics, worship and marital relations.
* Of capital and administration systems.
* Of education and call to God.
* Of religious commitment.

The evidence of all that is clear in the Holy Qur'an (The constitution of Muslims), which is a part of Muslims obligations, and they are supposed to consolidate the principles of moderation in themselves, their families as well as their communities and keep it away from extreme heresies and carelessness, so that Islam with its good objectives must not be offended or insulted.

Some examples of Moderation of Islam

♦ *Freedom of Creed:*

Islam had guarantees the freedom of creed and admits religious freedom, the fact which recognizes religious diversity as shown in so many verses of Holy Qur'an:

* (Let there be no compulsion in religion)
Su´ra: Bagara (256)

* (To you be your way, And to me mine)
Su´ra: Kafiru´n (6)

* (Let him who will, believe, and let him who will, reject (it)
Su´ra: Kahf´ (29)

♦ Not only that but Islam also guaranteed religious arguments a part from disputes or to be sarcastic of others, that the call to Islam is based on wisdom and beautiful preaching as the Holy Qur'an says:

*(Invite(all) to the way Of the lord with wisdom
And Beautiful preaching; And argue with them
In ways that are best)
Su´ra: Nahl´ (125)

♦ Islam also calls for dialogue between Muslims and Other people of the Book to come to common terms as the Holy Qur'an says:

* (Say: O, people Of the Book! Come
To common terms

As between us and you:
That we worship
None but God;
That we associate
No partners with him;
That we associate
No partners with him;
That we erect not,
From among ourselves,
Lords and patrons
Other than God."
I then they turn back,
Say ye: "Bear witness
That we (at least)
Are Muslims (bowing to God's will."
Su´ra:Āl-Imran(64)

♦ *Easiness of worship*

The tolerance and easiness of Islamic provisions are the most outstanding characteristics of Islamic legislations, which incorporate no difficulty or disaffection, but it incorporates kindness and good. So worship in Islam is easy that every man can do as Qur'an says:

(On no doth God
Place a burden greater
Than can bear.)
Su´ra: Bagara (286)

God has legislated worship with its easy provisions, God has also raised difficulties away from it, as Qur'an Says:

(He has chosen you, and has
Imposed no difficulties on you
In religion.)
Su´ra: Hajj (78)

♦ *Prayer:*

God has legislated the five prayers which are done by a special method, and in definite time and with specific performance. It includes rising, Sitting, kneeling and prostration. God has facilitated the performance of praying to be done sitting for those who are unable, if they couldn't, they are allowed to do it lying and if they couldn't they are allowed to do it by making a head signal even extent of raising eyebrows or even more by hurt. Ablusion must precede prayer for purification, but for the sick or the fatigued whereas water can cause them harm, or if they could not find it, God has allowed them to wash with clean sand or earth, as Qur'an says:

(And ye find no water,
Then take for yourselves
Clean sand or Earth)
Su´ra: Nisàa (43)

♦ *Zakat:*

In Islam, Zakat is regarded as the first systematic tax in the world history of economics. When Islam appear and imposed Zakat, the first step taken was how to arrange its collection, and appointed (defined) its specific ratios i.e. It should be levied at the rate of 2-1½ per annum on the total accumulated wealth of the country as well as on the invested capital. On agricultural produce, 10% are levied on lands. which are irrigated by natural means (rains) and 5% on irrigated land which require man's effort. And 2.5% is required on mineral products. The annual Zakat should also be levied at specified rate, on the herds of cattle owned by anyone beyond a certain minimum number. The amount collected of Zakat thus collected is to be spent on giving assistance to the poor, the orphans and indigent, passers-by, etc. Islam had also imposed it on the rich and those of average income, and named its expenditure as well. So, by these meanings Zakat is not only a financial system, but it is a worship for the capable Muslims to fulfill and naturally to be an approach to God and a response to the religious teachings. So, Zakat has become an inlet to social justice.

♦ *Fastening:*

God has prescribed fasting during the month of Ramadan every year, during which it is absolutely forbidden to eat, drink and keep a way from all appetites from dawn to sunset.

It is a worship, which is not confined to Muslims only, but it was prescribed on previous nations as Qur'an Says:

(O ye who believe!
Fasting is prescribed to you
As it was prescribed
To those before you,
That ye may (learn)
Self-restraint.)
Su´ra: Bagara (183)

Evidently, all religions practice fasting, but the difference between the fasting of Muslims and others, is that Muslims spend all daytime fasting, which is the normal working hours. To Muslims fasting aims at purifying and raising up souls to supply Muslims with a spiritual power. This is in addition to the other advantages which are hygienic, spiritual, social and educational which explain the easiness of fasting in Islam which permits the sick or travelers, to break fasting so as to compensate days later as God Says:

> *(But if any of you is ill,*
> *Or on a journey,*
> *The prescribed number*
> *(Should be made up)*
> *From days later)*
> **Su´ra: Bagara (184)**

Not only that, but pregnant or suckling women were permitted to breakfasting, so as to compensate other days later. As shown above, the four examples mentioned are out of five being the five pillars of the Religion. So, if Islam is moderate in issues concerning worship, it becomes logical as well that it well be moderate in all issues of life has we well see more examples about the intermediateness of Islam, the fact, which characterizes Islam from other religions ; the value, which attracted people to respond to its humanitarian Message.

Between universality of Islam and Globalization

The neutral view, necessitates stating facts about the two systems to determine either of the two is more suitable to mankind. It is not a comparison between the two, because Islam is a religion and that globalization is a new World Order susceptible to Islam, regarding it as an enemy, and accuseing it of violence terrorism and extremism. Islam as we have previously explained, had appeared fourteen centuries ago, and that it extended from the far East to Southern Europe forming the Islamic State and a Nation which contributed much to civilization. On the other hand, the Islamic Message was not only for the Arabs, but a universal one to all mankind on the earth. It's call is rich in mercy, piety and kindness. The prophet *(Peace be upon Him)* said;

(I am the messenger of "Allah (God) to you in
Particular (Arabs), and to all man kind)

Verily, Allah (God) the Almighty said:
(And We have sent you,
(O Muhammed) (Pease be upon Him)
Not but as a mercy for mankind
Jinn and all that exists)
Su´ra: AL-Anbiā (107)

Universality of Islam and its characteristics

And Islam is a humanitarian plan pivoted honoring man as one of its main objective.

♦ The respect of man, whoever he is, is an obligation
♦ The universal political system of Islam implies no domination to any nation towards another.
♦ The central universality of Islam, is in the service and development of its terminal points i.e. (Syria, Iraq, Egypt and Andalusia in Europe).Where the terminals which Islam had saved from civil wars and transferred them to centers of knowledge, wisdom and civilization.
♦ The universality of Islam had never an economic or political intention towards the occupied areas, but a right guidance and an advantage to the whole mankind, and the salvation of the weak and the down trodden on earth.
♦ Justice is the core of judgment.
♦ Dialogue is the basis of co-existence.
♦ Acceptance of diversity.
♦ Freedom of divergence.
♦ Suppressing factors of religious or section division.

Human rights and Democracy(Shura)

Islam was the first to call for human rights, concentrating on its protection of (human life, religion, mind, wealth and family), not only that but it is necessary to know that human rights in Islam is built on two principles:

♦ Equality between all mankind.
♦ Freedom to all mankind (based on the unity of the human origin, and the wholeness of dignity of all mankind). So, freedom in Islam includes all human freedoms (religions, political, civil, and freedom of thinking), and governance in Islam is based on justice and (Shura) democracy.

♦ **Peace In Islam**

There is a complete correspondence between Islam and peace, that, the term Islam is derived from the same origin itself from the term Islam which had been derived.

Allah has described Himself in Holly Qur'an, that He is Peace.

Holy Qur'an says:

> *"Their salutation on the Day*
> *They meet Him will be*
> *"Peace!"; and He has prepared for them A generous Reward"*
> **Su´ra: AhŻab (44)**

Allah (God) says:

> *(For (God's) forgiveness*
> *For them; and consult*
> *Them in affairs (of moment)*
> **Su´ra: ĀL-i-Imrān (159)**

♦ Obligation fulfillment is a morality which is not liable to bidding.
♦ Identities of others are respected and well kept and highly regarded.
♦ Environmental conservation, and development of the earth is a worship; and an obligation to use one's mind for the sake of mankind.

Allah (God) says:

> *(It is He who hath produced you*
> *From the earth and settled you)*
> **Su´ra: Hŭd (61)**

And He also says:

> *(And He has subjected*
> *To you, as from Him,*
> *All that is in the heavens*
> *And on earth: behold,*
> *In that are Signs indeed*
> *For those who reflect)*
> **Su´ra: Jāthiya (13)**

♦ Wealth in Islam is a means, taken from the rich and given to the poor and orphans, and regulated by moderate expenditure and chained by forbidding monopolization. So, in conclusion Islam as we have explained is a humanitarian economic, social and moral plan for life.

Globalization:

Globalization (The New World Order) has become a reality, but this phenomena has created a lot of fears and fearful obsessions due to its speedy process which changed the prevailing global atmosphere known. It is a new phase, with new facts reflecting a new global history. And as a human contribution, it includes both positive acceptable attributes and negative features refused by the global majority. From it is most important positive contributions are the means (the upbringing of the smart technology, communications, biotechnology and outburst of knowledge).

Why people refuse Globalization?

- ◆ The nation state is losing much of its sovereignty, because regionalization which is endeavoring to restore boundaries is confronted by globalization which is trying to penetrate and both of them are proclaiming against the state.
- ◆ Politically it depends on the principle: (Might is Right,) which means the neglection of International law.
- ◆ Culturally, it is destroying the structural values, interfering in the privacy of others so as to change the thoughtful, cultural, educational and ideological concepts of people
- ◆ It refuses cultural diversity with an attempt for an only one global behavioral pattern.
- ◆ Human rights of globalization is only a motto disengaged from the International law.
- ◆ Poverty, hunger and corruption are among the outstanding features of global economy. That is because only 20% of the world population are of wealth, and that 80% – the majority of the world population are living under the line of poverty, (in the darkness deep and social despair.)
- ◆ Monopolization of world economy, technology, knowledge, and mass destruction weapons.
- ◆ Environmentally, the industrial countries damage environment, and creating problems of global warming climate changes, and food crisis. So globalization is destroying both, man, earth, nature and cultures as well.

In conclusion, globalization is not totally to be discharged or accepted, but people want a responsible glabality, that of justice, equality, and of human and brotherhood advocacy.

Conclusion

The essence and fact of the humanistic thought is an activity to discover the unknown, progressing from the horizon of the known. Depending on this understanding we can distinguish between three forms of positive thought which confront the facts of the age in which we are living:

☼ The positive thought which confronts the age to which it belongs by analysis, exposition and evaluation, and attempting to uncover the elements of progress, supporting, and analyzing it, and then support the separation of all backward elements which hinder its advancement.

☼ The justification thought which is confined on the justification of reality and depending on it. But this type of thought is belonging to the field of thought figuratively and not factual. It will be better to those who believe in this type of thought to keep silent.

☼ The thought which is contented to withdraw with the historical and social reality to past ages. So, this type is not at all considered a thought. The multiple thought which we are searching for and trying to prove its validity from an Islamic perspective which comes within the frame of the unity of religion, but it is necessary to distinguish and separate between religion and the religious thought. This is because religion is a set of sacred fixed versions, while the religious thinking is a humanitarian endeavors to understand those versions, interpret and deduct its evidences. So, it is natural that these endeavors differ from one age to another, and from an environment to another too. The Islamic creed is not a new idea, but it is deeply rooted in history-it is the creed of IBRAHM, who named the Muslims before, and that Hanafia, Judaism and Christianity are but a one continuous religion with connected circles, and that the rising of Islam in Hijaz in the 7th Century A.D. was in reality a religious political, social and economic revolution, or to be more specific is a crucial transition in the history of the whole world. It is Islam, which contributed a refined standard of a civilized creation in many fields, and that its call for diversity is only but a forum of civilization, to know each other and interact from the differential situation which keeps to each civilization its identity. And in Islam as explained before – Intermediateness of Islam, remains beautiful, but it needs good understanding, and respect to others, that is because all people are brothers in humanity and facing the same destiny. So through dialogue people can easily avoid conflict and clash to pave the way for human co-existence. Finally I quote from Walt Whitman from his poem:(Splendour the Grass.)

"Though Nothing Can,
Bring Back the Hour,
Of Splendor on the Grass
And Glory to the Flower,
We will Grieve Not,
But Rather Find Strength,
In what Remains Behind"

Walt Witman

Glossary

Su´ra: Is a chapter of Holy Qur'an, built from verses, containing the Sayings of Allah ALMighty to His Messenger Muhammed (Peace be upon Him).

Hadyth: Is the prophetic sayings of the Prophet (Peace be upon Him). These Sayings concerning issues not mentioned in the Holy Qur'an, but actions taken by the Prophet, or approval of what He sees, heared or performed in front of Him.

Sharia: Islamic legal and moral code.

Call (Dawah):   Calling people to Islam through the best and most suitable means.

References

◊ The Holy Qur'an.
◊ The Prophetic Hadyth.
◊ Contemporary Islamic Visions, Al Arabi Book(45), July 2001
◊ Islam Confronting Campaigns of Distrust, Igraa Book, Dar AlMaarif, Cairo, April 2000.
◊ El Tayeb Ali A.Rahman, Globalization. Fate or a Choice, Khartoum,2002.
◊ The Present of the Islamic World and its contemporary Issues, Gamil Abd Allah, Riadah, Saudi Arabia, 2001
◊ Islamic Way of life, Abul A-Alaa ELMuwdudi.
◊ The Religion of Faith,Abdel Rahman Ben Hammad AL-Omer
◊ Islam On line and the Media.

Eltayeb Ali Abdelrahman

- Born 1943 in Sudan, Gazira State.

Education:
- Higher Certificate of Education-Egypt 1980.

Languages:
- Arabic and English

Professional Experience:
- Assistant Professor of Geography-Faculty of Education – University of Gazira 1994-1998.
- Registerar, Academic Affairs Secertary, AbuBaker Osman College Gazira – 2001-2004.
- Director of Culture – Gazira State 2004-2009.
- Secondary School Teacher-Geography 1966-1992.

Publications:
- Geography of the Nile Basin and Economic Development in the Sudan-1968.
- Globalization. Fate or a choice? 2001.
- Privatization in the Sudan – 2004.
- Submitted many papers, lectures in different fields.

Under Printing:
-Culture Between Two perspectives.
-Hantub Sec.School – Documentary Book.

Other:
- Member of many Non governmental Societies.
- Had Four Certificates of Benefit from Sudan and the Sultanate of Oman.